Magic Tricks
with Science

SUGAR

MATCHES

The Child's World

Published by The Child's World®
1980 Lookout Drive • Mankato, MN 56003-1705
800-599-READ • www.childsworld.com

Acknowledgments
The Child's World®: Mary Berendes, Publishing Director
Red Line Editorial: Editorial direction and production
The Design Lab: Design

Photographs ©: Gemenacom/Shutterstock Images, 4

ISBN: 978-1623235598
LCCN: 2013931438

Printed in the United States of America
Mankato, MN
July, 2013
PA02176

ABOUT THE AUTHOR

Samantha Bell is a children's writer, illustrator, teacher, and mom of four busy kids. Her articles, short stories, and poems have been published both online and in print, including magazines such as *Clubhouse Jr.*, *Learning through History*, *Boys' Quest*, and *Hopscotch for Girls*. She has also illustrated a number of picture books, including some of her own. For inspiration, she just has to turn to her family—there's always a story to tell!

ABOUT THE ILLUSTRATOR

Kelsey Oseid is an illustrator and graphic designer from Minneapolis, Minnesota. When she's not drawing, she likes to do craft projects, bake cookies, go on walks, and play with her two cats, Jamie and Fiona. You can find her work at www.kelseyoseid.com.

Table of Contents

Science Is Fun!	**4**
Obedient Eggs	**6**
Ice Fishing	**10**
A Sticky Situation	**12**
Eggstremely Strong	**14**
Waterproof Handkerchief	**16**
Wandering Water	**18**
Glossary	22
Learn More	23
Index	24

Science Is Fun!

Have you ever wanted to be a **magician**? Well, get ready to amaze your family and surprise your friends. With a little science, you can perform some fun magic tricks!

STAY SAFE

Magic tricks can be dangerous. Some of the tricks in this book use a candle or sharp objects. Ask an adult to be your assistant. Read each trick all the way through before you start. Then gather your supplies. Ask your adult assistant to help you find the best place to do the trick. Follow the directions for each trick. Clean up when you are finished.

Magicians use tools called **props** to help with their tricks.
Your adult assistant can help you get the props you need.
To perform the magic tricks in this book, you'll need:

- Shallow dish
- Eggs
- Sturdy, clear plastic cups
- Sugar
- Tablespoon
- Permanent marker
- Ice
- String
- Salt
- Water
- Balloon
- Clear tape

- Large pins
- Handkerchief
- Lump of clay
- Clear glass or jar
- Birthday candle
- Matches
- 3 heavy books
- Rubber band
- Shallow dish with a flat bottom
- Empty egg carton

WHAT YOU'LL NEED:

- A carton of eggs
- 2 clear plastic cups
- 4 to 5 tablespoons of sugar
- Permanent marker
- Water

Impress your friends by making two eggs obey your commands!

STEP 2

1 Fill each cup two-thirds of the way full with water.

2 Add four to five tablespoons of sugar to one of the cups. Stir it in until it is completely dissolved.

3 Put an egg in the sugar-water cup. Make sure it floats. If it doesn't, just add more sugar.

4 Take the egg out. Then place the two cups on a table. But remember which cup has the sugar! It's time to bring in the audience!

STEP
3

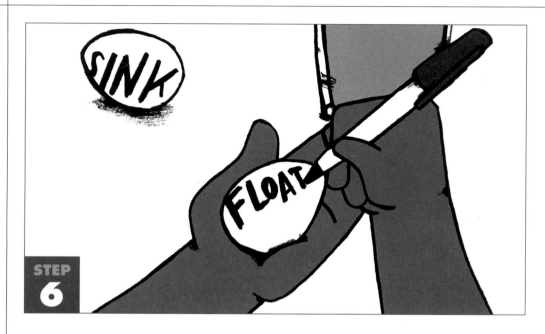

5 Ask someone from the audience to choose two eggs from the carton.

6 Write the word *sink* on one egg with your marker. Write the word *float* on the other egg. Tell the audience these eggs will obey you!

7 Place the egg with the word *sink* in the cup with the plain water. The egg will sink.

STEP 8

WHAT REALLY HAPPENED? Have you ever noticed that you seem to weigh less when you swim? That's because the water pushes you upward. This force is called **buoyancy**. Adding sugar to the water created more buoyancy, so the egg floated.

8 Next place the *float* egg in the cup with the water and sugar. This egg will float!

Your audience will be amazed!

- 1 ice cube
- String
- Salt
- 1 cup of water
- Shallow dish

Ice Fishing

Get ready to show off your catch with this next trick.

STEP
3

1 Tell your audience you can pick up a piece of ice with only a string.

2 First place the ice cube in a shallow dish.

3 Then dip about one inch (2.5 cm) of one end of the string into the cup of water.

4 Put the wet end of the string on the ice cube.

STEP 5

5 Now just sprinkle some salt on top of the string. Say a magic word.

6 Wait about 20 seconds. Then pick up the string.

You'll shock your audience when you pick up the ice cube, too!

STEP 6

WHAT REALLY HAPPENED?
Water becomes ice at 32 degrees Fahrenheit (0°C). This temperature is called its **freezing point**. Salt helps lower water's freezing point. When you sprinkled salt on the ice, it started to melt. The string sunk into the ice. Then the ice quickly froze again around the wet string. The ice cube was stuck to the string.

A Sticky Situation

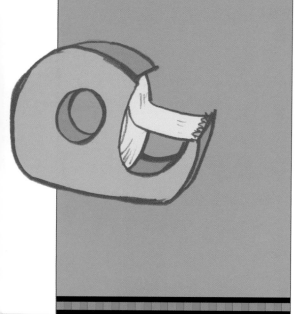

Everyone knows that balloons and sharp objects don't mix. Stick a balloon with pins in this next trick. Your audience will be amazed when the balloon doesn't pop!

STEP
2

1 Start out by blowing up the balloon. Then carefully tie it off.

2 Place two pieces of clear tape near each other on one side of the balloon near the top. Then turn the balloon. Make sure you can see the tape, but your audience

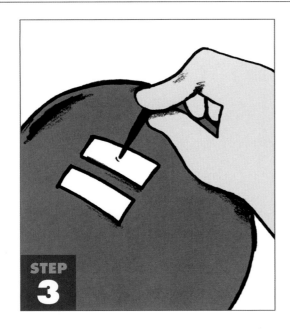

STEP 3

cannot. Now bring in the audience.

3 Pick up the first pin. Slowly stick it in the middle of one of the pieces of tape. Push the pin halfway into the balloon.

4 Now put the second pin into the second piece of tape.

5 Let's end with a bang! Pull out one of the pins. Poke the side of the balloon, and pop it!

STEP 5

WHAT REALLY HAPPENED?
Like everything, balloons are made of tiny **molecules**. The molecules are linked together. This makes chains that stretch. But if the molecule chains stretch too far, they will break. The balloon will pop. The tape kept the molecule chains from stretching too much, so they didn't break.

Eggstremely Strong

For your next trick, you will pile heavy books on top of eggs without a single crack!

STEP 1

1 Begin by placing the eggs in the four corners of the egg carton. Make sure the eggs all have the pointy end up.

2 Tell the audience these four eggs will hold up a stack of books.

3 Now pick up the first book. Lay it on top of the eggs. The eggs won't break!

4 Pick up the second book. Lay it carefully on top of the first book.

5 Then pick up the third book. Lay it on top of the second book.

Your fragile eggs are magically strong!

WHAT REALLY HAPPENED?
The secret of this trick is the shape of the egg. Each egg is curved like an **arch**. The strongest points of an arch are at the top and bottom. The books are sitting on the strongest part of the eggs' arches.

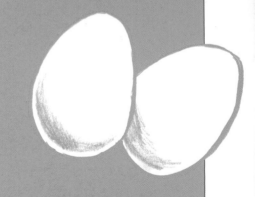

- Sturdy, clear plastic cup
- Handkerchief
- 1 cup of water
- Rubber band

Waterproof Handkerchief

Impress your friends and family with this handy hanky.

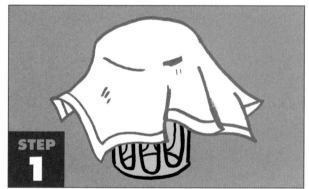

1 First place the handkerchief loosely over the top of the plastic cup.

2 Prove that the fabric is not waterproof. Slowly pour water through the handkerchief and into the cup.

STEP 3

3 Next pull the wet fabric tightly over the lid of the cup. Put the rubber band over the cloth. This will hold the cloth on tight.

4 Now flip the cup over. The water won't come out!

Your audience might want you to tell them how you did this amazing trick. But remember, true magicians never tell their secrets!

STEP 4

WHAT REALLY HAPPENED?
Water is made up of tiny molecules. Water molecules tend to stick together if they can. First the fabric was dry and loose. The water had nothing to stick to. It went through the holes in the fabric. Then the fabric was stretched tightly and wet. The water molecules could stick to one another. This created a **membrane**. The membrane filled in the fabric's holes!

Wandering Water

WHAT YOU'LL NEED:

- Adult assistant
- Shallow dish with a flat bottom
- Lump of clay
- Clear glass or jar
- Birthday candle
- Matches
- Water

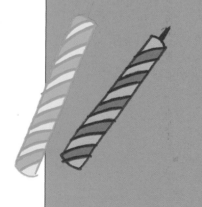

In this next trick, you can make water flow upward! This trick uses a lit candle. So make sure to get an adult's help!

STEP
1

1 Pour some water into the dish. Place the dish on a table. Tell your audience that you are going to move water from the dish to the glass. You will do it without touching either one.

2 Next put the lump of clay in the center of the dish. Put the birthday candle in the clay.

STEP
2

3 With the help of an adult, carefully light the candle with the matches.

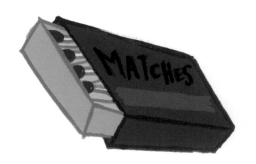

4 Then cover the candle with the glass.

As the candle burned, it heated the air inside the glass. The air cooled when the flame went out. Cool air takes up less space than warm air. There was room for the water to come in. The burning flame also used up the oxygen in the glass. The **air pressure** in the glass became less than outside of the glass. The outside air with the greater pressure pushed the water to where there was lower pressure.

5 The candle will soon go out without any air. When the candle goes out, some of the water will move up into the glass.

Amazing!

Glossary

air pressure (AIR PRESH-ur): Air pressure is the force of air pressing on a surface. Burning a flame inside of a glass can change the air pressure inside the glass.

arch (AHRCH): An arch is a curved design used to hold up weight. Eggs have an arch shape that makes them sturdy.

audience (AW-dee-uhns): An audience is the group of people who watch your tricks. Practice your tricks before showing them to an audience.

buoyancy (BOI-yuhnt-see): An object's ability to float in liquid is its buoyancy. Adding sugar to water can increase the buoyancy of an egg.

freezing point (FREEZ-ing POINT): The temperature at which a liquid changes to a solid is that liquid's freezing point. The freezing point of water is 32 degrees Fahrenheit (0°C).

magician (muh-JISH-uhn): A magician is a person who performs magic tricks. True magicians never reveal their secrets.

membrane (MEM-brane): A membrane is a thin layer of material that protects or covers something. The water in a soaked handkerchief forms a membrane that prevents water from leaking out of the handkerchief.

molecules (MAH-luh-kyoolz): Molecules are the smallest parts a substance can be divided into while still remaining that substance. Water molecules tend to stick together.

props (PRAHPZ): Props are items used in a performance. Gather your props before practicing a trick.

Learn More

Books

Buttitta, Hope. *It's Not Magic, It's Science!* New York: Lark Books, 2005.

Spangler, Steve. *Fire Bubbles and Exploding Toothpaste: More Unforgettable Experiments that Make Science Fun.* Austin: Greenleaf Book Group, 2011.

Web Sites

Visit our Web site for links about magic tricks with science: *childsworld.com/links*

Note to Parents, Teachers, and Librarians: We routinely verify our Web links to make sure they are safe and active sites. So encourage your readers to check them out!

Index

adult help, 4, 5, 18, 20
air pressure, 21
arches, 15
audience, 5, 7–9, 10–11,
    12–13, 14, 17, 18

balloons, 5, 12–13
birthday candles, 4, 5,
    18–21
books, 5, 14–15
buoyancy, 9

clay, 5, 18, 19
cleaning up, 4

eggs, 5, 6–9, 14–15

freezing point, 11

handkerchief, 5, 16–17

ice, 5, 10–11

matches, 5, 18, 20
membranes, 17
molecules, 13, 17

permanent markers, 5, 6, 8
pins, 5, 12–13

practice, 5
props, 5, 6, 10, 12, 14, 16,
    18

safety, 4
salt, 5, 10, 11
string, 5, 10–11
sugar, 5, 6–7, 9

tape, 5, 12–13

water, 5, 6–9, 10, 16–17,
    18, 21

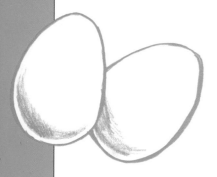